SONG OF MY SOFTENING

SONG OF MY SOFTENING

OMOTARA JAMES

Alice James Books
NEW GLOUCESTER, MAINE
alicejamesbooks.org

10 9 8 7 6 5 4 3 2 1

Alice James Books are published by Alice James Poetry Cooperative, Inc.

Alice James Books
Auburn Hall
60 Pineland Drive, Suite 206
New Gloucester, ME 04260
www.alicejamesbooks.org

Library of Congress Cataloging-in-Publication Data

Names: James, Omotara, author.
Title: Song of my softening / Omotara James.
Description: New Gloucester, ME : Alice James Books, [2024]
Identifiers: LCCN 2022009297 (print) | LCCN 2022009298 (ebook) | ISBN
   9781948579247 (trade paperback) | ISBN 9781948579483 (epub)
Subjects: LCGFT: Poetry.
Classification: LCC PS3610.A4498 S66 2024 (print) | LCC PS3610.A4498
   (ebook) | DDC 811/.6--dc23/eng/20220224
LC record available at https://lccn.loc.gov/2022009297
LC ebook record available at https://lccn.loc.gov/2022009298

Alice James Books gratefully acknowledges support from individual donors, private
foundations, and the National Endowment for the Arts.

ART WORKS.
arts.gov

Cover art: Image by Noma Osula

CONTENTS

PART TWO: THE FEAST

I. Drum

II. Wind

III. Piano

For my mother, who made sure…

I was a late bloomer. But anyone who blooms at all, ever, is very lucky.

—SHARON OLDS

Prologue to a Name

THE BODY IS an unmarked grave before it is given a name.

On the seventh day, all gather 'round the newborn in purpose,

in ceremony. Elders, parents, kin and priest assemble the necessary

ingredients for a life. Place them on her tongue. Bring sugar,

if you wish her to know sweetness. Honey, in case the sugar is so sweet

she spits. What child rejects the slink of honey. Salt,

as there is goodness in all things. Alligator pepper, so her life

shan't be too plain or *ata ire*, for fertility. Water, for it has no enemy.

Obi or kola nut, ensures the girl will *no iku danu*. One taste and

she will vomit death away. *Orogbo*, or bitter kola, and she shall

grow ripe with age. Now, the child is ready:

PART ONE
THE SACRIFICE

I. BRASS

Having No Grief to Speak Of

I giggled with the world
cooed in its ear

Held hands
I sat down with the world
laid down with it

Mulled about and romped
rolled over

For it, I made of myself a world
and swelled

Bearing it alone, I laboured,
squealed, heaved

Bore it all   My body
a new source of life   I carried
it on my back, around my neck,

upon my shoulders
Nurtured it from every neglect
I suffered, searching for tenderness

I cleaved myself from it, for freedom
is the birthright of every being

Where there was indifference
I, first shelter, then tunnel,
bridged it

as it came and went
—as love is wont—

until the unthinkable animal bit,
severing us, as it spat language
leaving me with only words

and none of them enough

Half Girl, Then Elegy

Having fallen while no one was looking
Having borne what fell through
Having fallen early

/

Having barely fallen through myself
My luck, so close to catching
Having caught the worst of it

/

Having fallen from the sky and then
Through it. Having landed to realise
I had been part

/

Having parted the late sky, partly
Sky where I am delicate, I took
A tumble through the night bloom

/

I took the night with me as I tumbled
Delicate with the infinite
Which swells from the tallest branch

/

Having grown swollen
As low-hanging fruit, I tell Nadra
I couldn't help it—

/

The fresh heave of new breast
Thick switch of hip: a group
Of unnamed gifts is called a steal

/

She says fruit you can reach is still
Precious. Her name means *rare*: her lean
Thins towards the unusual

/

In Lagos, we name our girls
Darling, *Sincere*, *Precious*, because
A name is a stake in the grave

/

Having grieved and taken and taken
On the way to Eros, Thanatos
Having arrived late to my own bloom

Halve me like a walnut
Pry the part of me that is hollow
From the part that yields fruit.

Twice a Month on Sundays with Maxine, My Tender Head and the Truth

There are things only a hot comb and your mama can tell you
about yourself. Sorry, but you better listen, child. Sure, it's hard

to stand up on that block that leaves nothing to the imagination.
I had to damn well invent my own escape. Who wants to rub tits

with the truth, morning, noon and night. That shit ain't
consensual. You bet ter tough en up. Otherwise, I pity the meal

this world is gonna make of you. You'll be sliding ass-first
off the jagged tooth of some knuckle-headed fool and soon,

unless you hatch a plan, girlie. Sh ooooooo t. Now be still,
so I can press those roots.

Autobiography of Thud
After Donika Kelly

You live in Elmont, New York,
in a small house with a big yard
and gate that doesn't lock.
Have a best friend
with shiny black hair
called Clarissa, who shares everything
and might be the only person
to smile when she sees you.
You play at her house after school.
She is not as brown or round,
but that doesn't make her more or less
beautiful than you, just likable.
You take the bus to school Mondays-Fridays,
where you almost always share a seat twice
the width of your *womanly* hips, unless
someone is sick and no one wants the seat
next to you, where you practice how to leave
your body. You daydream
that your mum doesn't have to work
and sometimes you're sure you see her
powder blue car trailing the bus, from the window.
You don't wear glasses, but think they look smart.
Can still look people in the eye
when you speak and are spoken to.
Unsupervised adults, busy boys and girls
have things to say about your *figure*, which
is the word men are most likely to use
when addressing a growing girl. *Trauma*
isn't a word you've heard anywhere, including
on the playground or the tele. Instead, you pick
up pretty junk, like muddy flower barrettes and strange coins.
Your pockets jangle on the bus home with your private
collection. You strew your loves with abandon

across the kitchen counter. Clarissa shines them,
placing them next to the repurposed tin can
on her dresser. Neither one of you knows the word *altar*
or wears the fancy barrettes to school.
Your mother works overnight. Your father too.
But his Aramis follows her Opium parfum
like the sun does the moon. In the morning,
the near miss of his body seems easier.
You roam like a buffalo through his possessions.
Spritz his cologne. Finger his ties. You could be anyone.
Mom shouts the warning for the bus. Reality
returns to the tongue like dry cud. You trot
through the kitchen to graze in peace, where
you find a different, familiar island gyal.
Every six months, maybe, dad brings one in need
of work before she travels back home. They
watch you and your brother. Closely. Discern that
Trinidad is not *your* home. You awake to girls
in the shape of women towering over you.
They are as mean as square-cut glass. Get up
for school. They remind you how you are *American*,
which you learn is slur for fat. They leave.
They return six months later with mangos,
black rum cake and small parcels. They teach you
fatty-fatty boom-boom is the sound you make
when you walk, when you smile or enter
a room: *fatty-fatty boom-boom*.
You don't know how to fight,
but have instincts to protect your brother
against people he won't remember.
You prize him. Your secret is
that you have usurped his real mother. You play
Candy Land and Monopoly. Your brother
loves money so much that you trade him
pink and blue bills for Halloween candy.
You are aware you like food more
than you're supposed to. You unwrap the candy

beneath your pillow so the sound doesn't carry.
The first day at camp, your training bra is discovered
by Jessica Rosen in the locker room.
Who accuses you of weighing 100 pounds.
Who washes her hair every day
and smells like flowers before they die.

Untouched

Although I wouldn't learn the word *consent* until years later, the way it was explained to us has never betrayed me, rather, is the inkwell I dip my pen into, to push past all erasure, all would-be, invasive narrators.

That day of 4th grade, when Natasha came into class and inadvertently told us she had been touched by a family member, she wanted to know if she was still a virgin.

Our favourite Quaker school teacher, Mrs. Kern, looked into her child eyes and said yes. Immediately. Said, virginity is something you give, not something that can be taken. That someone has to ask your permission. That up until the day you say *yes*, you are a virgin.

The spell of these words would bind my life, with their good and merciful magic. Open the portal of the world back up to me, as I stayed silent. Silent with sisterhood. Mrs. Kern held Natasha, as we all formed a circle of arms around her.

This definition of consent would bridge the gap between the me, violently unseen, to me, in the world, fumbling towards hypervisibility.

What our teacher instructed was what I had already begun to learn, earlier, in the 1st grade of Gotham Ave, and what I would finally put words to decades later: the word yes. How it was more powerful than the word *no* when someone is on top of you.

So much love to discover. With my first lesbian lover, I was so overwhelmed by what I had said yes to, by the consensuality of it, that I stopped in the middle, put on my clothes and needed a break. She asked if I was joking, as I exited the bedroom, leaving my desire in the other room and sat down next to the girl I was, at Gotham Avenue.

No one talked to her about the boys who chased the girls, throbbing through the hallways at school, past empty rooms and combination lockers where she sprinted for her life, turning right, sometimes left for the atrium.

The unspoken fear, without an orator, an invisible tangible thread, like the vibrations from the treads of their soles, scuffing the linoleum, hunting the v-word she'd never heard, the quick breath and muscular friction of their clumsy hands, over then under the brown sash of the Brownies uniform she was made to wear Tuesdays and Thursdays, a show of school spirit.

She used to love to run, to chase the blood of her thighs, not the boys, who preferred her still beneath them, and swollen, with silence of seedlings desperate to sprout, as they took turns gleefully reaping,

digging their fingers into her soft brown flesh, breaking in her new breasts and twisting her nipples (hard) like they were turning earth, like it was their rite to pull those girls through that passage, in public.

In private, my lover perplexed and satisfied, in the next room, I recall the first prod, the first pinch of my fat in his flat fingers. The surprise of his nails, like ice, like the first frost or heavy snowfall of memory,

when my good mother bundled my brother and me, voluminous in our snowsuits, preparing us for the inclement weather, as the forecast called for heavy precipitation.

I never think of what it was like for the other girls. I don't imagine their small, soft faces. I don't care what they show in the movies, when soldiers leave the field, they don't go out drinking with each other. When they pack up for home they know, for this lifetime, they have seen enough of each other.

Connection, a precarious barometer, I remember the great blizzard of my youth. I was breathless with laughter, falling face-first, into feet of snow, walking home from the bus stop with my brother, also laughing, as I cried, unable to get back up, my snowsuit protecting me from nothing.

My Father Remarks That I Prioritise My Nigerian Heritage over My Caribbean Side

I tell Joe I have no grace. I mean I cried unashamed an entire day for a
woman whose wife is with child. For a woman I no longer love. I tell
you I would cross the street today to avoid her, without looking back.
NO! Joe says he doesn't believe in the *not looking*. The young beak of
the past still draws blood beneath the old feathers. Joe says these bullshit
theories of closure are poor substitute for mercy—which is all my
mother could give a child, guilty of nothing, born between my brother
& I, whose light-skinned mother flew her down from Canada. How she
must have yearned for him. Her first official visit to her father's house.
House father was reluctant to enter. A young girl left to strangers. A mother
left to children. A witness left to remember. Three birds, one stone, but
oh, how large. The bird of his in-between daughter abandoned to our
strangerness for a week & mamabird, whose grace also wavers in
inclement weather, did nothing less than kneel beside his lanky
offspring, sick from dinner or absence. Bowing, beak to beak. Two
jewels, crowning the toilet seat. Small, Black Afro-cut diamond of a
woman, mamabird, stroking the innocent cheek of my father's
indecision, with her sturdy, unbrokenwing. The kiss of betrayal still wet
on her cheek. Mothertongue sucking back suffering, only to bend to
sisterbird with a kiss. Mama, whose long ago stepcreature tried to push
her daughterbody out a moving car and into the bad part of town so my
smallboned mama would suffer. Suffer as only smallwinged birds can
in the maw of this hard-beaked world. World constructed to undaughter
one birdbody after another. NO. Mama learned early to bend even as she
breaks. Mother now, with her good wing around the bird I don't call
sister. Both my wings clutching the brother who doesn't enter the poem
until this second, & my lovely follicles, falling soft as snow above the
nest I carry, nothing to catch them as I write this.

Wall

In the evening, I remind Bruce
to shut the door to the closet
because the kitten already knows

a door is a wall you cannot climb
you must walk through.
Yesterday

I promised Jennifer
I was over you,
then logged into

your Instagram,
counted backwards
to the last photo of us

trying on dresses
like I used to
with my mother

who promised to tell the truth
especially when it wasn't pretty.
One day, I remember

leaving the mall
with a bag full of bras
and grabbing her

hand on the escalator
resting my head on her shoulder.
I was ten

when she let go
saying, *People will
think we're lesbians.*

Sometimes
around 4am
my full stomach

growls like the kitten
paws at the door
she can't claw through—

in every house
a room
for the unknown.

Haircut

When I tell my mother I am in love with a woman. She looks up from the frying pan and I look down as she asks me what it is that we do. She means sexually. She wants details. I think it's time to invest in coconuts. Never learned to stomach the smell of my mother's palm oil inside her American kitchen. Announcing itself in hot splatters across the clean lines of the cold porcelain. I still lay my temple across a cool surface, splay my troubles atop a tiled floor. Limbs like I'm seven again, naked from the waist, beneath my mother's steady hand and long silver scissors. Which always feel like surprise ice against my chubby pubis. Eyes pinned east beneath her impatient voice. *I said don't move.* My girlhood, open as the morning blinds, the light I wish was brighter. When Mama's finished cutting, she dusts the loose hairs like a janitor, underpaid. Sighs. Now I'm allowed to be a girl again. Pull up my shorts to play. Outside the air tastes like honeysuckle and I am on the cusp of forgetting. Until she calls me home. I pretend not to hear her questions. She wants to know where I am going.

Markers

Suzanne's back in the hospital for cutting. I wince
as Shola relaxes a clenched fist. Sucking smoke
he says, For *cutting*. Don't worry, I say, she'll return
soon. This place might do the trick. Shola exhales,
the trick. Repeats. The trick. Asks, what is the trick
to not cutting yourself open. I shift. Closed tight
inside my skin. The light brown rings 'round my belly
expand into a burn. Again burn 'round my thighs and
backside. Again burn the parabola of my calves. I mind
the burnt flags of my arms I almost never unfurl. Singe
them against the cold hood of Shola's car. Beneath us,
the engine croaks as Johnny croons about the burning
ring of fire, on repeat, my body,
taut balloon, cradled in fleshwire.

Ceremony

How do I love[1] this body?
Cradle it in gauze, like a third-
degree burn? My mother loves[2] my fat
to be covered, specifically
the affected areas:
arms, belly, back and thighs.
The darker the meat, the more
vulnerable to light. Her hands,
the first to sheathe and swaddle.
Her wrists, weaving the inaugural
spells. Her fingers, holding the spoon
I open my mouth to tell the story
of wound. Poem, I am lost inside you.
How do I begin again? Wo[3] counsels
to imagine the portal that leads home,
what it might look like. I think: sun.
I see: shadowy basement doorframe,
mandalas of mold and the ex-lover[4]
who said she loved[5] how her skin looked
against mine. Who devoured my dark
fruit like a worm. Who spews my light
silk, still. Can one ever undo a spell?
Part of my father believes
I might still be a doctor, a model
or both. His foggy eyes a-glitter with
the sparkle of an infinitely crushed
mirror. You see, he fancies himself
a sculptor. Tells me my proportions

---

[1] see: *enter*
[2] see: *applies pressure to or requires*
[3] see: *one synonymous with love*
[4] see: *usurper of truth*
[5] see: *by comparison*

are perfect. Would love[6] to see me
finally do it. Damn it. Love[7] myself
enough to lose—loosen what hangs
around my masterpiece. Gazing
across the whole of me, he grins
every time, *it is your time*.

[6] see: *imagine his triumph*
[7] see: honour

Promise

When they send the robot to replace me, do not be gentle with it. Place these chords where its heart chakra should be. Do not speak to it of a fountain—tell it, in the middle of its life there will be a flower: a blooming, petalled trauma. Tell it, I considered beauty, once, but there were white-iced, gingerbread cookies, brown with molasses, in the ceramic, Black Santa jar. My father's mangoes, green, red and yellow, were in a wooden bowl on the kitchen counter, unharmed, having traveled so far beyond their home. There were the last hours before sleep, when mother borrowed energy from the next day to make at least three nights' worth of dinners for us. Until the night roused me with more night and I masticated with tongue. Masticated with teeth. Masticated in my sleeping gown. Masticated beneath the sheets. Masticated in the bathroom stalls at school so quiet you wouldn't hear me over the sound of a raindrop. I am a master-cator. I will masticate. Until there's nothing. Until I'm full. Until I'm done.

Things
I know to be true,
but will never prove
For Annette Kern

that
when someone you love
dies

you get to call
"dibs"
on your slab

duet
requires a partner:
someone

to record the message,
limp
the 3 blocks to Home Depot,

purchase
the small objects, tools that cut
God's

large plumelike panicles
off
the hollow reed, so it might

sing.

My mother's nerves are shot—

a nerve is a shot. A shot
is an arch. My mother is an archer.
The archer breaks the dead branch dead.
Dead branches rot. Rot from the bark.
My mother's nerves bark: shot
through death. Death peels her nerves.
Death is an archer. Death shoots rot:
just misses her. I see her tremble.
Moss greens her bark. Greens where she
trembles. Where there was death, fruit grows.
The fruits of death. Fruits moss the branches
through the blinds where she trembles still.

More

I went to the hardware store for milk and you weren't there
so I went to the graveyard for eggs
but just missed you. Then I followed the waterfall
of your perfume down the railroad track,
but couldn't lift it. There aren't any flowers
at the steel mill or the lumberyard. Out here,
even the air burns from the
near miss. Even the moon
needs a cool sip before
illuminating the evening. I
hardly ever have a partner
when I go walking—oh,
how your nearness
incites the grieving.

Proverb

You must cut your coat by your waist,
you preach, when you catch me
reaching for a dress outside my budget,
as if it were a *cookie*, which we all know

was my first word. Not *Mama*.
Even when we don't discuss
gastric bypass,
we do.

You ask if I am afraid
of the knife and I chuckle,
for I have been long-groomed
for the blade. Anyway,

it is not for me to say
how brave   only
that I would peel back
the fresh scabs

like a potato skin
drag the slotted blade
across the surface
from syllable to line

one at a time
West to East
then West again,
if it would urge you

to grease the pan.
What if the body

is just the throwaway,
the spotted frailty
that barely drapes:
the words

we are unable say.
The leftover love,
no longer appropriate
to plate.

a little tenderness

my first word was not *mama*, but *cookie*
i don't make a lot of money
could be more beautiful
remain fat
my mother doesn't understand my friends
the aesthetics of my expanding flesh
she might understand why i don't love men
but not how i've come to love women
or why i cry
my mother, never taught me to understand her
in her native language of Yoruba, her language
was providing a *better life*, she stays busy
surviving what we took without thinking
twice, my mother avoids complexities

from my writing chair i can still hear her
the length of her befuddlement is as long
and winding as all my years, heavy as hardship
private as disappointment, the distance of her arm's
length is precisely how much she loves me
i imagine her, often, as a girl
denied the outstretched arms of a mother
to keep her safe, or someone to convince her—
while the window was still open, while
she was a soft child with unblemished hope,
countenance still as palm oil, before it's fired
—that she was perfect

Perfect.

i spend my nights on the internet, looking
up words in the dark, practice my pronunciation
i know i'm not doing it right, i give up, this
is not how you learn a language, i catch

a reflection of myself on the dark screen,
left to cope with the facts of life and a loving God
on my face, the look of bewilderment,
she's worried for my heart while i'm worried
for my heart

First Kiss / Under Capitalism

When I learned I had power to build
on this market, I took it. The currency
placed on the mouth
of a seventeen-year-old girl is startling
to the girl herself. Child of the 80s, I understood
you don't get anything for free, baby.
So when the brother of my best friend
reached gently for my right hand and
placed it, delicately, with his left—
the way one might set linens and china
on the table for an important guest
—atop his hard dick
after I'd just helped him fold his family's laundry,
I saw an opportunity. A wrestler at school,
I knew he would follow me up the stairs
because he liked to practice pinning me.
Already the autumn of my senior year, I was afraid
of what leaving high school with untouched
lips might indicate about my human capital.
Understand, when I pulled my hand away,
to retreat from the den to the upstairs kitchen,
this was not an act of self-preservation
but exhilaration. A private minute.
I told myself I was ready
when he found me, held my waist and walked me
into the family pantry, where he asked me
to suck his dick. Presumably a standard deviation
of the market. I said, *I've never even been kissed.*
He pushed his weight on top of me, my body
knocking the parcels off the pantry shelves.
It was almost over as soon as it began, when he pressed
again, pulling it out, before I had a chance to consider
whether or not it was worth a first kiss. I guess
it was better than nothing, even if I had to haggle for it.

Ice Sculpture

My heart:
A mosaic mass of bundles and fibres and weakness
Gathering every half second out of loneliness,
Then finding shame, loneliness, then shame,
Failure, then shame, sorrow, then—
Poems of ice convert the loss,
Exaggerate the melting
Pulse.

Mama Wata

The saliva seeps from the glands at the base of my tongue
the way the earth rejects the rain after (or worse)
during the flood. Pursed lips seal in the fluid.

My tongue   womb-ly   like a baby
sinking
further from consciousness back into the amnio.
This
is a warning.

Whereas

from girlhood, my mother taught me to fear
public restrooms, driving in the city
early-onset womanliness and compliments
from strange men,

because a mother loves like milk
sours
on the kitchen counter | at noon | inside your locker | at 2am

but a father's love
provides metaphor
in | oncoming | traffic,
rots you to the root—

is a soft candy sucked
hard against the molar
complicit
in sweetness

a father wants justice
to press hard
against the man who rapes his daughter,

whereas a mother
knows no justice
except a mother's love

On Repetition

No one gives a damn about a poem
until they need a poem. The poet
is a poem. My mother is a poem.
Women are poems. Black women
are poems. Black people are poems
who need poems. Black labour is a
poem another person will say they
wrote. Black babies are weeds.
No one thinks a fat person is a poem.
At most, an anthem. Disability poems
can be read when an abled person says so.
The urge toward poetry is a type of soil.
A Black death is a poem we clamour to
sing. What I said before about Black people
is a half poem. Black intellect is a diving
board. A wellspring. A tornado. A patient
lava. Black poems show you everything
about the world you claim to love. Love
is a muscle the poem exercises, or not.
A weed in the mouth of the poem is a fruit.

Moose / Leaving Philadelphia

Cruising up the Vermont mountain the evening I,
at the centre of my breaking, do not die, midnight
drives my small sedan almost vertical. Atop the icy
steep dark, a feeling louder than intuition
and more dense than the surrounding fog, gathers. I brake—
stretch my heel into the pedal, a chill sits me upright
in my seat as the wheels skid to stop. I am at the peak
of something greater than my gasp and then nothing.
Cold silence. I see two pairs of legs. Heavenwards: belly.
A sneeze is all it would take for me, an unabsorbed droplet,
to slide past the meniscus of this life into the next. This
is it. The feeling you wonder about the whole time. I feel only
the numb dumb foot of my birth trembling hard against the metal
and the thick pads of my mother's mother's mother's mother's
mother's mother's fingers around my neck, steadying me
so I do not cross. Before me, always, an entrance

Rufus, I never met you, but I want to tell you

For Rufus Wainright

this cup
(you can't see it)
could be my brother
or my sister

it's empty
but you can still see the ring inside
the height
to which a thing within its walls could rise
before leaking
out the bottom

you have two choices:
to believe nothing
or everything I tell you

did I have a choice
when a stranger
the Bible tells me is my brother
picked me up
with a sweet smile and clammy palms
to drink me

tell me yes and I'll sing Hallelujah
pick up that cup over here there
(one with the smears' could be my sister)
and smash her

Dissociation in a Time of Cuffing Season

Escaping the occupied apartment
where nobody loves her

for the bruisegrip and thrust
of November night

this body, tossed 'cross the starlit back roads,

below Nick Drake's heavyplump
trembling,

she opens her good blouse
to you, pink moon, as you sink

your bottom lip into this chest,
gravel beneath her shoulder

blade a sharp cradle, rocking us
'til we're soft with knowing

nobody loves you when you're down and out. Even now,

beneath this twin blanket
I write this.

Outside, the futile winds,

and this moment where nothing gets in—
not a chest cold, nothing,

this high tide season
our bare feet, shivering.

Equilibrium as the Day After

Making my peace with yesterday
for dragging me shoeless
through the hours without you,

you return, as the wing of a butterfly
returns to greet its twin, briefly
and in flight. Soulself, I have missed

the blink of you beneath my breath,
fruit that flowers in my fist
a kiss to mark the divine boundary

betwixt shit and soil. I have loved you
every day with a resistance
I have spared my enemies.

Bang and a Whimper

A Black mother will tell you,
with a straight face and stretched belly, that she didn't want you to be a statistic.
Math makes a poet of us all. Made me homeland and diaspora. Half ship and half sea.
Love catches up to loss, eventually, follows the arc of failure. What I am trying to say is
mathematical. The fragment of hope implies the fractal imagination: a multiplication
of feathers behind what the eye reads and the mind perceives. Reader,
I have been picked up, put down and considered, casually and constantly, which is the
privilege of beauty. I have two origin stories. I don't know who I am. For every new flag, an old
suffering. Let the fire consume as much as it wants. This ruin could be anything. No
more barkwood, cane or papyrus. I was not made to bear fruit. A stye in the eye of glory.
I have two origin stories. I know who I am, born of an earlier god, praised
for my natural geometry. My enemy bends me at the waist: minute, barbed wire blossom.
I do not know winter. Innocence survives everything. My only tree bears fruit.
I was the original.

II. STRING

A Mother Can See More Sitting Down than a Child Standing Up
|Yoruba Proverb|

1.

My mother looks at me as I am no witness to myself
the summer before college, eighteen, when she states
in the mirror, that no man will ever love me
at this weight. The tears I don't cry
(then) mean I am not too weak
to receive such honesty.
Maybe she is more
right than we
dare to
see.

2.

Sky—
and what
about woman.
When I return after
years away, after months
of silence, Mom barely looks at me.
When I tell her I was raped, she can barely
whisper it was a good thing she didn't raise me in Nigeria.
I look to her. Want to douse her in my tear-shaped arms, fat, like
a heavy blanket: the weighted kind they make special, for folks who have trouble
looking you in the eye. Or being touched. But I don't. Touch her. Or ask her to explain.

3.

Mama I'm going to sit by the river,
& eat Jollof from the pot.
Come with me.

Homosexual

adjective

1. (of a person) sexually attracted to people of one's own sex.

(of my father), before he left, saying we come from good stock, which was how I imagined our dead, not as friendly ghosts, but as inheritance pulped in their graves, softening up this earth, long after their stakes bowed or they had anything left to sow. Having returned to my father, my childhood seeds gone to pulp, his firstborn's face shaped by what Yorubas call *wahala*, my spring blooms stilled, sagging from the stem. Buds bursting with time, but firmly closed. (of the island of Trinidad), I watch my father remove the sandals from his feet, dipping his toes through me as if into the family plot. As if he is traveling back to the first photograph of us, at the beach: a man, guarding his daughter's return to the water that nearly claimed her. A girl, without foliage, fearing the heart's watery call. Having become incredulous to the tilth of knowledge. (of a home) where I did not speak until spoken to, in this blue-green water, clear as glass, I am expected to characterise these feelings flowering for my lover. I don't say that I love her. Father knows imagination doesn't germinate from nothing. (of my T'auntie's ivy), still wrapping itself around the rusted, iron swing, decades after she went down for her dirt nap, having never married. In her prime, it would have been the sixties. Sexual revolution. A poet tills for context: a bone meal abandoned to the elements: the snow, the heat, the detritus.

Triolet

/Love/is more thicker/than forget/
/No one asks/yet/always arrives/here/
/You leave me/to walk through walls/but bet
/love is/more thicker than/Forget
this fur/these ears/wag/my nose so wet/
/with want/waiting/bent knife through pear/
/Love is/more thicker/than/forget/
/No one asks/yet always/arrives here/

Exhibition of the Queered Woman

you said
you'd *turned* me

just as
you'd turned

others,
women who'd loved

you before,
you meant *changed*

which is
an active verb

to shift form
or state, or colour

Δ

in nature
specifically fall

when we say
leaves turn

what we mean
is *die*

which is
synonymous

with *become*
i came

to crave your
begging

me to stay
through

your states
of illness, your

open and broken
marriages,

Δ

we exchanged
promises

without
audience

before begging
off

i was wrong
to think

i understood
how

the wheels
in your head

turned
the act

of moving
in circular direction

around an axis
was always

the point

Δ

in water

switch from low
to high tide

signals
seabirds

to forage
at night

Δ

the fault
turned out

to be
mine, my turn

now, as in
opportunity,

to break
for sanity

to swallow
bruise

that begins
in dark blue

lurching towards
context

The Butcher: A Love Poem

Since you've returned
I have imagined myself decapitated
Inside a meat locker, strung upside down
Hanging silent as a painting.

Cold metal hook through the anus,
Cleanly gutted, the blood: fresh
But not dripping,

Red circles
Where my wrists and ankles
Once were, suggest contact

And then, you walk into the freezer
Where you leave your signature in bone,
Like a fingerprint on a canvas still wet.

In spite of all the damage, your blade
Remains sharp. Loose skin and fat
Lie in piles at your feet.

Like roses, uneven stanzas or enjambments
Even now, I belong to you
And you to me.

Sonnet of the Bull

A bull killed itself on a wooden post after being sent into a terrified frenzy when its horns were set on fire in front of a baying crowd.

—*The Independent*

The only woman I ever loved came with an army
of strangers to kill me, so I made myself a star.

My pads cracking the cobbled streets free
of the past. We began as two animals running (free),

but our fat days burned thin beneath the wide eye of grief.
Had I not outpaced the delicate body of my birth,

she might have never noticed me. Alas,
one forgoes the rescue of love.

When your lover is the matador and your soul mate, the sunless rage.
The chase, the only stroke of pleasure to part you with soft hands.

Hot breath on the heels of your final gallop, then bam, *Bull despairs
amidst the frenzy and dies instantly.* Death, a picture made of light,

sings for me. Because love croons like a surprise torch of fire.
Because love comes for your horns.

White Cliffs of Dover

No one asks the water as it opens for the body
        to welcome what it guzzles to its grave.
Lagos holds my first memory of being lapped
by abundance, Bar Beach. My feet, drumbeats
disappearing into the shore. This day I am safe
enough, with family, but next time I sink into
the lap of a sinking sand, my lover holds me
under, longer than I have breath, my tongue
bowing the notations of her heartbeat. Who thinks
to ask the siren what she knows of silence. No one
asks the water why she opens for the body, or what
she welcomes, as she carries thrum with wave. I
scry another word for *forward*, having learned
too late to resist tucking myself between a woman
and her lunacy. She, who will do to you, what she does
to herself, fool, as you place your neck in the maw
of her brokenness. She will lie about the taste, say
you persuaded her to bite down, as she tooths you,
        smirking as she swallows.

Fruit Flies
For Madeline

At the top
of the list of things
we never talked about.

                    Could never talk about
                              at the top
                              of your list.

Is the baby
was
the baby.

                    How long did we keep him
                              1 day
                            was it 3?

The life
of the average fruit fly
spans s e v e n:

                              7 days
                in average conditions.
                    In optimal climates,

could be forty.
Might reach fifty.
Definitely.

                              Not.
                              3.

Before you found me,
how many days
of wanting.

                        Did you whittle
                            down
                            to 3?

I watched you
carry him back
through the same

                                                                    doors
                                                      as 3 days before
                                                               today,

without a say.
In Nigeria
seven days

                                            is when the Yorubas gather
                                                    around the baby,
                                                     give him a name.

But Madeline,
you and I
know the truth.

                                                          About the lives
                                                                  that
                                                               perish.

Inless
thanoptimal
conditions.

Mirror Talk

For Madeline

the woman who faked cancer
was the first

                             to reap the secrets
                                 of your body

her knowing hands
firmly turned

                                   your flesh
                              into an orchard

every way one can lie
in beauty & truth

                            she studied, or stole
                               'til the soil

dried yellow &
the stems hollowed

                     this season's harvest moon
                            an empty plate

before you
left her

                              you forgave
                       her hollering *fat fuck*

the night she left you
in the car to swallow pills

                       your bottom barely fit
into the chair beside her hospital bed

she never said sorry
or meant it

                            when she cried
                          all the fruit dried

& the days got shorter
& you got fatter

                         with brokenness
                    fatter with predators

your thighs
expanding into the night

Shame

If I am ugly, my ugliness straddles your knuckles and your bite
If I am ugly, my ugliness takes the shape of your mouth
If I am ugly, my ugliness be the hue you don't glow

Morbid Subtraction

if I lose
a hundred pounds
i'll still be fat

Δ

if i lose
two hundred pounds
i'll still look fat

Δ

if i lose
three hundred pounds
i'll still feel fat

Δ

if i lose
four hundred pounds
they'll say, that bitch was *fat*

Heaven Be a Sturdy Chair

When I show up
to the reading, it's not
to talk to you. I'm cruising
for stability. A pound of fat is three times
larger than muscle. Fat
demands space. Describes it.
Fat belts a show tune, plus
an R&B, plus a ballad
at karaoke. My fat
never goes home alone. Think
about your last moment
of pleasure.

Multiply it by three.

Δ

the only rooms I occupy
are empty

at my annual appointment

when i'm asked to disrobe
and talk about what's happened

with my body. you see
everyone travels through

some sort of prism   atsomepoint

Δ

in the shower, i travel to the far regions

to forget
her predilections

for internet gore, theway
she'd question me

about the rape. thesteam
choking my throat, never mind

its effect on the skin. anyway
what is fire until it burns you,

but comfort

Δ

at the theatre

i don't watch Tyler Perry movies
bc i was the only girl in middle school

with the-colour-brown skin
bc students & teachers assumed

so where in Brooklyn
when Brooklyn meant brownskin

bc my parents paid full tuition

bc the adults insisted

bc the well-intentioned white people suggested

bc the cool girls said i

bc all the boys, yes *all* the boys knew

i should be grateful

Δ

maybe, when a fat Black dyke is president

Δ

Optimus Prime, the Tooth Fairy and White Jesus
walk into a bar...

When I said I had Obamacare, what I meant was *Medicaid*

Know I should
but can't articulate
that *down and out*
nobody wants to talk about

that *nobody wants you*
nobody needs you Nina thing
she could sing out. I
can't wrap my taffy head around

that Cholera in the over-there water
nobody over here gives a damn about.
That I-don't-want-a-cigarette, but
can ring the smoke in my throat

type of lowdown. That
trouble that flips,
vaults, then lands faith
back into her place, so

she moves up from JV
sorta thing. What
is this aching fiber-
ous breast trying to say?

Doesn't matter, anyway.
Sprain a memory,
drag it through a rhyme,
call it poetry

in that thick-lipped
let me pleasure you, don't
worry-about-me-self-
less-type-way.

Biopsy

you used my hands to trace the map
where you said they'd taken the cancer
from your gallbladder

the melted chocolate ice cream scar
that looked like a spoon burned into your belly
still visits the parched mouth of my dreams

two years ago
you said you had two years
to live,

new year's eve
you came clean

during visiting hours in psych
claimed that the truth
drove you to insanity

Δ

Years later it would take two pairs of legs and four arms
to escort me into the ER

something had ruptured inside me
i thought:
this is it

from inside the stirrups, yelping
as the gynecologist scraped me
with the dedication reserved for the bottom of the yoghurt cup

for a week, discoloured grey bits
and pads of blood flee
the extra thick lining of my uterus

now
the eggs i have left are playing tricks—
learned possibly from the lies your whispered into me

because i cannot reach your womb
with my tongue,
i bite my lips

My therapist says i am angry.

Δ

i wanted to believe that you left
the carrion of love unharmed
i was wrong

You Are Not Brave: A Female Utterance

I concede
there is an art
in recalling
the familiar
over and over.

I once watched
a long-necked
short-legged crane
g r a z e.

You think it's easy
to balance that way,
what little it was able
to carry was worth
at least double
its weight. Let
this short-lined
frivolous poem
p a r a d e
downwind
of sentiment.

Yes,
those who are born
to us
deserve to be
named.

Say again,
Don't you want a child
and I will answer.

Either way
when I'm gone
what will be left
but a rough estimate of my name?

Closure

My parents were scheduled to divorce on Valentine's Day.
I was there in the beginning, sat next to my grandmother

in her teal blue dress and hot combed strands. As a rule,
she refused to appear unrefined. In a warm church in Trinidad,

a wedding evening in hurricane season, we wore our Sunday best,
my mother and I, in matching white lace and wide eyes.

Why shouldn't this bond be marked by an angel with an arrow,
tasked to put an end to the sorrow of suffering alone

love meant to be shared. The sugar apples of my mother's cheeks,
rouged more than the red carnation pinned to my father's smokey

blue suit. I search his handsome jaw and boyish grin for clues. We keep
the happy secrets of these fleeting Trade winds, in the family album,

so old, the memory and the artefact have become one. Pigment sealed
to plastic for eternity, a reality that cannot be undone or loosened,

only destroyed. Marriage is a valentine that misses me,
though I have imagined myself able to walk up the aisle,

if not back down it, which is partly why I was disappointed
when the court rescheduled without a reason. Perhaps

the judge on the docket, newly in love, refused to chance the karma
of divorce court. I can say it now, these years later,

I was eager to be asked to witness our family's legal dissolution.
The annihilation of vows that were broken. Tell me

what's louder: the pluck of the arrow, or the bang of the gavel,
or the ever-lasting gaze of the first-born daughter.

You call Ky in the middle of the night,

say, you don't want to die childless
on the toilet, like uncle so-and-so,

who probably wasn't a blood uncle. Open
secret. He didn't look a thing

like grandfather, though he wanted it, terribly—
died clutching the name of the family

he regularly condemned. My therapist says
depressive thoughts are circular: a spinning top,

stopped. The trek of childhood resentment, deliberate.
Canned tuna in your pack. A single change of socks.

You wake up laughing. Funny, how death
hunches across the hour. After midnight you rummage

Al Gore's internet for generosity. Research DIY wills.
Call your best friend. Your studio, mostly dark. Ask her

to be your executor. Imagine your things spinning
across the globe without you. Uncle died fighting

for more, until there was nothing. No assets.
No property. No tension where flesh meets bone.

The body's final act is giving. Mother said,
it was a week before they smelled him rotting.

In Lieu of Ode

For Tarana Burke

When you are fat and queer and female and black
When no one has any use for you except
Your otherness

When your otherness is a currency
When no one wants what you're selling
Because your price is too high

When your high is self-respect
When you are alone
And the bar feels low

And you are not rich
And you are not KWEEN
And you are not it

Not three fifths—
A dime piece,
Not new to this.

When you have no better offer
Than to bargain with anaphora,
Abandon yourself:

To a new name, cut, wig, weave,
To a new book of poems, creed or country.
To anyone who heard Tarana say:

No one can take what was meant for us.
It can be used by everybody
and still be ours.

The Good News

Because I believe you cannot stop a thing from existing
even if you kill it
is how I loved you

Because in my thickest vibrato I sing for Sarah
even though she cannot hear me
is how I loved you

Because I crouch under the tilted sky
even as these knees choke on their age
is how I loved you

Because rain melts the February snow   renders the sun redundant
even if it's just because I say so
is how I loved you

Because my tongue points true north
even with this mouth of ghosts and hard swallows
is how I loved you

Because   is how I loved you
Even   is how I loved you
is how

I am Resistant to Trust

My GPS
The local news
My appetite
A man's touch
Beauty
The last avocado on the shelf

A promise
Especially if it is mine
Especially if I want to please you
My need to please

My therapist
When she suggests I try
Something new

That Karma
Has updated the latest version

The results
Of the blood test
Of the vote

My own touch

Anyone without a song—
Anyone who sings

That it's not too late

The antidote
A second look, which lacks
The integrity of a stare

The last bite or first rush
of blood

Proper Fat

Thin with disgust
     Fat with wordless joy
And patience

Thin like the opening of the gate
     You pray you'll make it through
Fat like the other side

Fat with pubescence
     With moonstone or pearl
Thin protection

Fat as the ripe earth, before it was turned
     The black soil, a dense fruit, unwavering

The fat trench of the womb
     You share with your sisters

Fat like forgiveness and
     God's Grace that delivers you
From the enemy of yourself

     Proper fat

Fat like a second, third and fourth chance
     As the number of tries it takes
For you to finally get right

Dear, don't mistake generous for infinite
     Every abundance that can be chewed,
        Can be expelled

Fat like the girl you always knew you were
     The fat redemption

Hope, the innocence they couldn't kill, swells
    With its daughter

A Flair for Language

She wasn't easy, is a thing we say

about someone we love. My father

says this about his mother. Grandmother's

words could *cut you from the far side*

of a room, well into her last years.

The expressions on her face were widely

reported. It wasn't necessarily the content

of the opinion, although, it was sometimes,

but how it was packaged and delivered

to your door. One might say she had a *flair*

for language, if it was a Trini ole-talking.

Which is why I had little choice but to laugh,

one of the last times I saw her,

lustrous as velvet in her dark brown flesh,

recalling me, under the glare of early dementia,

as a *lovely little darkie*, in a more fragile

voice than the one bellowing into my girlhood,

Fatty-Fatty-Boom-Boom. Her smile hanging

off the long vowel, like a cat's tail, upturned

to the moon. You see; it's a miracle I still love

rhyme, the coincidence of language and time.

Moving to Brooklyn during the Peak of a Pandemic

My people,
born to lick joy off the dragon tongue of despair,

don't hold out our hands for gifts—we
gift each other.

While you were moving to the suburbs and I,
still tending your garden of secrets

and unforgivable crimes,
almost died, but wouldn't.

Hear me:
I tender no reward for your violence.

Three Women / Two Transfers and a Token / One Reincarnation
For Max Ritvo

Lately
flossing in the sink or
tweezing on the toilet

or hovering over the pregnant woman
I gave my seat to
when I haven't been touched in months

I stare into my reflection: into my mouth
towards the fleshy back   See life
evaporate into nothing—

a hole where there was *ivory*
once   and I sink like a cavity
into the soft tissue of time

as it is proof of all we cannot repeat   Ecstatically

a woman's baby gurgles
above the engine and the heat   I shift
my eyes   Open my mouth   Make sounds.

PART TWO

THE FEAST

I. DRUM

Said Sorrow to Joy

After Kahlil Gibran

What stands between us
the hours
never parted

when you were a soft
nothing
molten   child,

I blew you to bubble
to bulb,
to bloom

yawned
the paradigm of time
into the weak fire of light

I made you
synonymous
'til my knees bowed

carried and hoarded
the original ode
tight-lipped, heavy-lunged

Do you remember
what you were singing
when Kahlil renamed you

in breath
dressed you with language
adorned you in prayer

when I was the first
to suffer
barely blown and bastard, I

hushed your hardly-husked
first flesh
shucked and shucked   and finally

you
you
you

Bodies Like Oceans

For Shoog McDaniel

Spare me your thin tidings
        bring round your unsolicited fats
Your baby fat, your tired fat
        fat of the evening tide
Fat of the early worm
        bring me that stubborn belly
Fat of the unspoken
        underserved and unrequited
Pocked, puckered and long-pummeled
        fat-on-fat-on-fat fat
Flesh, that responds to touch,
         jiggles at the suggestion
A provocation of fat, tested
         to withstand the fallow ire. Please,
Don't mention the memory
        of muscle without the tensile tenure—
Long live the cross-legged splendour
        of fat privilege. Oh, slender stride,
Whom do you comfort, with your ease
        whose borders drape across your back?
Clawed my way out
        of your clean love
And into the world's fat shine
        world that works to burn
Me, I stay alive and well
        rounded at every corner
Keep your thin spectacle,
        your airy hula hoop
Fat of the forgotten republic
        I lift you out of the shade
Let your contours spill over with light
        I offer not the lemon,
But the sour grove as heaven.

Poem to Watch over You

The day you were born was the shortest of the year or the longest,
there was a rain storm or hail or it was a cloudy or cloudless night
and your mother or your birth mother or your father or your birth
father or your life giver was reading at home, was on their way
back from the store was on their way to work, had no place to go,
was dreaming of you when you woke them, when it was time,
when you were ready to arrive, to escape, to see what the fuss was
about. On the way to the hospital, on the way home, on the way to
the midwife, or the bathtub, in the back of the ambulance, taxi
or parking lot, on the side of a hill, we received you, pulled you
through, held you, made an opening and whispered, shouted, urged,
pleaded. You are welcome, you are welcome, you are welcome.
There were no requirements nor identification nor documentation,
you were born without restriction. Not even the supernatural could
hold you back, bold thing, from this oblivion.

Tides

On the toilet
I think about my students
who can't agree

       how to *define* gentrification

       only how it feels

       dense / yellow / ochre

s i n k i n g

       like a shofar
       into the throat of the bowl

       waste complicates ritual

       creates layers
       of listening

when Leonard Cohen hums

       you want it darker

       from his starry throne

       earthworms bristle
       in burrows

       stretch to the surface

release anchors

       u n d e r g r o u n d

       tides
       of invertebrate vibrato

Pier 52
After a photograph by Alvin Baltrop

He looks through the wound of my life like it's light. So I let him. The last cube of ice. Outside the tray. Where I found him. My lover. Melts atop this brick, as if it's our last whiskey together. His brown, more fragrant, more dangerous than whiskey. You couldn't miss him. Nothing lasts. Of promise. Such is the promise of light. Not even day breaks between us. Black joy, cresting over and over the summer sun. Kept a spiral of his hair, in a box, like a favour. His favourite pair of trainers. The taste of his lips where we first kissed. Where we first blissed. I couldn't— though I tried. To keep him. Wouldn't keep. Still. Nor true. Keep up. How could he keep me, when he refused to keep time? Didn't keep me in compliments. Was I supposed to keep sweet? Look. We discovered day like it was fire. Flesh, like empire. Touch like bloodlight. Yes. Count me down like a missile. As of tomorrow and the day after. As of this darkening gelatin and silver. As of the moon and the monsoon rain. As of these piers. As of America and all its splendour. As of the alleyway and the archive. As of this F-stop. And this fuck. And the next. As of this click and shutter. As of the daffodil and every queer thing that obliterates winter.

Black Art Sonnet in Which Lines Were Shuffled and Glued

Because Black folx know the feeling

Of being cut into strips and re-glued

I must stop my hands from reaching

While I gaze at a collage I

Position them behind my back as I peer,

Do I look a figure in his eye? Keep a hand in my pocket,

Enact the colours, the cutting, the shapes?

Should I mirror the black outline?

Hand on my hip, or gaze past the frame of him?

Romare Bearden said art is the soul of the people.

My borrowed face, my grandmother's almond eye

Critiquing the masterpiece of myself that ain't new

Face of a borrowed boy looking back at me,

T(his) queer unblinking existence

Portrait of an Uncaged Child on Easter

To the small child wearing the bowl-cut
Crown of hair as a-burden
Open blue puffer-jacket
And wrinkled collar-shirt
Performing a fit of boy-ness
Splaying your back-body
Across the window of the deli-counter
Like a Jesus under-study
Named for your short-stature
Maybe puny-Peter
Unable to ignore the-pull
Of gravity across the im-material
On line with your apathetic-mother
Who's apparently stopped even-caring
About your mid-day
Silent out-bursts,
Not yet pu-bes-cent
Old enough to know-better
Than your well behaved sis-ter
Wearing her petti-coat
Like a han-ger
While food-shopping
At the food-market
On Easter Sun-day,
You are-right
To-scream
Bloody-murder
Even the tender-loins
Beneath the glass-agree
It's 2019 in A-mer-i-ca
And a bad-time
To be a small-thing

Tripartite

(White)

I want to sing, America,
but my teeth fall back into my throat,
a darkness of flesh and hollow

the way a stolen song returns to the sea.
No, no, I cannot sing America,
my music rather die than bear your trouble,

but trouble
is a thing larger than the form
it occupies, so you understand

that I have always been troubled
by this hunger
this desire

by sex
Blackness
and my own tenderness, endless

plummet into untilled land.
I don't know what day it is,
but it is 2:30 somewhere in America

June, 2020
and I call Sahar to say,
I am a hot mess. By now she knows

to ignore my Americanisms, her delight
undetectable on the phone, daughters
of foreign tongues, we queer joy

privately. The way she taught me to
pronounce her name, *Sahar, rhymes with "hair."*
What is it about June? I think

if I die tomorrow, I want her
to speak for me. When she asks
how I am, she already knows, says,

You are holding a lot. Her mouth,
too full of a mother's kindness. The kind
my mother was never allowed to know. Softness

is a sacrament, placed under the tongue.
The tangles, dread up inside me,
root indiscernible from shaft,

indiscernible from coil whispering
into my bed at night, *Nobody loves you.*
Afrofuturist, because not in my lifetime.

(Blue)

I open myself at night and try to root
out the violence. This will take
time. Root, which implies ground,
which implies dig, which implies snout.
The root of all evil is want, as in the want
of a man with a sword and shield,
begetting a man with a gun and shield. The moan
in my mouth travels the route of my
bad tooth, which implies pull up by the—
or rootless, a sound so close to ruthless
between my gap. Tooth, a word that connotes
root, is imbedded in the body, in its
structure. The structural root of my
sorrow, of my blues, was born out
of Germanic etymology, or history,

which means violence, and not my
body. I am not a Black body, but
a being, which implies unencumbered
by you.

(Red)

Sahar, I am completely suspect,
instead of doing any of the work
I should've done today: I ate Jollof
rice, two bowls, haven't showered,

wrote a poem, Googled my ex,
Googled my ex's wife and child. Have
done no housework. Watched reality
TV. Ignored texts from my mother.

Wrote a bad poem that is not really a poem.
Avoided emails. Googled myself. Found one
of my poems on a website for song
lyrics. My first love was song, though

I never looked the part. No
one chose me to front their band, so
I sang on my own, thinking of that
jazz singer, Blossom Dearie,

discovered long after her bloom.
Having bloomed early, having
missed it too, my eye, always
fixed on the gloam of August

and the fruit of late summer.
It is mid-June and my sisters are
disappearing. My brothers, brown
ivory, dangling by the root. And this country,

only meant to be an offshoot,
can't carry a tune. We scroll the screens
of news together. Blood on every finger,
tip to root. Unlike nature, words carry half

-truths. I am holding *off*,
or staving infection. Never been able
to love a thing straight on, only from the side,
soft, damp rot of mess, hot beneath the skin.

What We Leave Undone

The ukulele from Honolulu
has yet to be tuned & I

thought I'd surely learn
to play a song

before she took a wife.

The year Theo divorced David,
he taught himself to play guitar

for survival, he said.
I just needed to save myself

the repetition

of a broken heart,
which is a workshop

for
what might have been.

//

The salve of watching my mother sleep, spreads cool, like a family who knows

little of violence. This, the reason
I never tell her

of hands, ten feet outside our gate

reaching from the open doors of a Cadillac, maybe
if not for those large, sunken seats

or the driver's uneven sense of time
—what they could have grabbed,

fistfuls of baby fat.

//

A healing balm requires shaved beeswax
placed into a pan, over low heat.

//

I lock the silent gate on my way to school & wait carefully at the curb.

When I see a dark Cadillac, pee pours warm

like infused oil, into the pan, melts
over the wax. If those older boys had reached me,

the way my mother reached across
the ocean & landed with a dream,

I do not know if I would have screamed ( )

//

Across the waters from Nigeria, I see
the headlines of the Chibok girls

who go unnamed as a conjuring. I read:
Schoolgirls Abducted, then Child Brides, then On the Anniversary of....

They, who were marked unlucky & then unlucky & then unlucky

I want to tell—
but only, oil & beeswax ( )

//

In prayer, I open my mouth to their dreams & hear
myself scream.

//

At night,
I leave the salve, top open, on the nightstand by the haunted strings

for the ghosts,
who exist for no reason

but to finish these things.

Ars Diaspora with Drinking Gourd
After Richie Havens

As morning unspools new glory across the earth, it rescinds an inch
at least, of borrowed light. Today those who wake heavy and heaved

beneath the lowest rung of love, press their ears to the first quail calls
of sky. I ride the train north, underground, having hollowed the enemy

of its gourd-mouthed pride. My father's gaze across my flesh measures
the distance between my life and the grandfather I never met, on Earth.

The evening before I arrive, my father's father, disembodied by time,
visits him in Trinidad. The Caroni River of my father's tide surges,

eversweet, a sorrow runing through the sugar belt. He recalls the dream's
wordless joy, my granddad smiling ahead of me. Today, we are headed

into New York City, rare luxury, to dwindle time. Stripes of shadow
and light play the width of my father's face, brown, dappled black.

The present moment: a ribbon, a slideshow, a conjuring of tenses
we emerge from, pulls tunnel through light. Dad dips back into memory,

like an acrobat, to find a young man's posture, shifting in his vinyl train seat.
He recalls granddad's face, a map of my birth, each dark twinkle of his eye,

a dead tree, summoning. Yesterday's grief has traveled on ahead of us,
between two hills, a haunting where love waits. Dad says, our dead return

when the flesh is weak, to remind or warn against— each beginning
and ending, a landmark. Tonight, midsummer sits, across the moon's unset table:

the meek yet to inherit the earth, the suffering yet to end in peace. Upon me,
the measureless distance between words I need to believe, and what spirit has

always perceived. Parched of favour, I follow the drinking gourd. I call and call and call and call and call and call and call. When conducting the music of the departed,

thirst hums the gospel of the body. I almost always lose my way. Dark, my most loyal friend, sings only me.

To the Mother of the Boy Found Floating Asleep on the Lake

For Naya Rivera

Do not despair this motherless sail,
dear unsailed mother, your boy sleeps
safe. Hands have found him. Wrapped a
blanket 'round. Just yesterday
he sailed through your earthly waters, you
still the water and the hand that guides his route.
Sleepy distance between love and land. Between
now and then. The break of death, never far, mother.
Mother him, from the lake of slumber, into which
he'll nightly plunge. The sailing sleep of death
only parts you from your vessel, not your boy. Love
is still the sailless voyage home.

Ode to Extinction

where there is no God
only content
death is not enough

when I die I want
my poems to die too   I want
every ungodly word

to unknit any trespass against—
my body to unbody any healing
rendered holy and the wound

will remain unnamed
wound as eye, I reopen

II. WIND

Got 'Til It's Gone

After a Mark Romanek video with Janet Jackson, feat. Q-Tip & Joni Mitchell

We pivot like we pray—for no gaze. Only Black shines
in its darkness and light, by which I mean on and on and on...
Like steam, music be how the message bodies to the sky
is what I see in Janet's smile. She, brown and glittered golden,
leathered in cool. Q-Tip on the beat and Joni Mitchell never lies:
Black be the thing you can never quantify. Catch us kissing
and mending our bodies in the blue black. Catch us blasting and
Dutty Wining in the lamplight, the summer Miss Jackson teaches
rhyme to hug its own line. My back bending, twisted t'ward sorrow
all that time

         waiting, for song to arrive.

Body Image

No matter how they

try to claim you, your body

can never belong to them. It will

always be ours. Piece by piece

I made you whole with my love,

shaped you to share with

the world. I gave you unbroken,

portion of my portion. This body, your

sacred text and map back to me.

However you fall, fail,

submit to frailty, your body

cannot conceal the message. My love,

you are the message.

Museum of What Is Owed

The walls lining the exit of this life and entrance into the next
will be lined with all the art inaccessible to this body.

There will be letters, framed and signed, by all who loved me
secretly, out of convenience, for fetish or sport.

There will be installations: video, visual, fresco, mixed media,
for every unwanted hour I survived being unwanted.

Before we arrive at apology, let us stroll the hall of acknowledgment.
Before a Black child can be loved, she must be seen

and before a Black gxrl can be seen as beautiful, she must be acknowledged.
For a Black woman to be acknowledged,

she must be claimed by a community and honoured.
The honour of Black womanhood resides behind a glass case

at the centre of the intersection, of *We Do Not Live Single-Issue Lives*
and *All Roads Lead Back to Heaven*. There is always glass everywhere.

Heaven on earth is a patient woman with time to spare.
My good mother with her good heart spared me every pain

she absorbed from the mallet handed down from generation of man
to generation. My mother is a busy woman. No time to create

a found piece when she works 12-hour shifts, so I collect the shards,
tend to their inanimate needs. Line the white gallery walls with what

cannot be counted by the hand,
a smithereen of glass, a joyful gxrl, a grain of sand.

Mixed Media Portrait with Hard Subjects and My Mother's Soft Tendencies

When I conjure of my mother's softest parts.

The pout her lips make when she's decided to take you into her heart, she'll call you as if she's reminding herself, *sweetheart*. It's not a term of endearment, but a notice that you can rest and she's ready to take on what you can't carry.

The slight shoulders of her small frame shying away from all the love she deserved.

A lap that smelled of all the perfumes of our childhoods, because that's the kind of woman she was. French powdered puffs and designer eaux de parfums: gifts from Aunties and Uncles visiting on their international trips, purchased at the duty-free shoppes, on layover.

Because under everything, she is feminine, with a capital "F."

When I glance back to record the small algorithm of my birth, I see
mum was braver then than I am now. There are those who make the history and there are those who record it. Those who live through it and those who live with it.

Black Woman Gets a Massage:
Has Discourse with God

I ask: is pain grief, leaving the body?

If so, freshly-seeded trauma stay close.
Call it: shuffle, limp, waddle, I drag
the earth with me as I walk, the spirits
of my dead stay fresh on my heels
the mud of my sins in the corner,
stay on my boots.
The masseur tells me it's safe to sleep
and I dream of Florida. Frozen
iguanas fall from the trees. I carry them
to the river to be reborn, but there are
no fish to bless, just plastic, as the sea
rises to swallow.
In the throat of the dream I forget to wake
before I die and you tell me to bring my own chair
if I want a seat in heaven. *No save-sies.*

I return to the table, alive on my birthday.
Return to the body as the scene of grief.
You sing Happy Birthday and I ask
what do you mean? Say: mortality
is a heaving saturnalia. Say: death,
like the art of photography, works with
what's inside the frame. You say: pain,
the light leak across the composition of time,
adding as it subtracts.

I think: aesthetics are not facts.
My boots there, in the corner, dry.
My muscles flicker with dimly lit room.
A single hand palming the fat, over the muscle
of this poem, again. And again. And.

After the Last Calorie of the Apocalypse / Prayer for the Clinically Obese

On the last day, let there be a fat inhalation
of delight between the lap of our sunrise.

As the tongue separates the doubt from the cream,
let pleasure sift through the metal strainer of time. Only

hours now. Waiting for the thin people in my life to die,
I read a magazine, have sex, smoke a cigarette and

ride the elevator down to the lobby. We've only minutes
now. Having nothing against them, personally, unlike art

they don't improve much upon the original form. Why
was I only ever awake to the past, my past selves asleep

to what was plentiful? Exiting the lobby for the corner
store, I pass an absurdity of them. Only seconds now, staunchly

insisting their last instance be tailored to fit. Their paper lips
fanning the tulle hem of my dress, red, for the rest of us,

mere moments away from freedom, from this fine tyranny. If only
for a short while, as they begin to shrivel and wilt. Oh

mercy of the thin breeze. On this day, lovelies, we will be free
when the food runs out.

Direct Objects

The Supreme Court legislates my body, in pieces.
I court the wings of the quarter note. Jesus rose
after three days, they say, the end is closer than
the beginning. Supremacy is a thing that rises in place
of itself. How close to danger was He, on the thirty-
ninth day? The term for a stranger duped twice is
a fool. The word for one who agrees to suffer
a fool, is teacher, the way a rose can teach the bush
that what survives winter is as mighty as what endures
for just a day. Did they look for Him on the fortieth day?
My mother averts her eyes when she asks
what I plan to do about it. My diaphragm belts a note
from its sleeping quarters. Because my mother slept
ready for the belt, she had no patience in her voice
when she'd wake me. Unbroken, I broke
the cycle that reared me. They say He died gladly
for all of our sins. I fooled myself with the force
of my own love. My hips are wider than my mama's
patience. My dead leave breadcrumbs beneath my feet
at night. Darlene's last words were, *I don't know
what to tell you*, then she died the next day, in a doorway.
What is death but a hoax we punctuate: a comma
that ascends to crown the head of memory, that takes
both the left and right hand of the father, folding
one into the other.

Allāhu Akbar:
for my body
under the rule
of white supremacy

go ahead and cry
go ahead and tweet
ignore / delete / devour
everything you can
fit onto a tongue
go ahead lie, uncover
or seek cover

go ahead and hold
your breath
walking in brown skin

past a murder
of men / a flock /
a congress / this
year's insurgents

on the North Lawn
in the subway
outside mosque
at first light

just around
the bend
leap ahead and
breathe underwater

lay down your words
desegregate your heart
pick up Lucille Clifton
recall the language you live in
part your six-winged seraphim
call them to sing

on your knees
on your back
on your feet
go where the love is
The Greatest

Notebook Full of Thirst for the New Year

After Lucille Clifton

hacks the hard beaks off the birds
who fed from my hand   kisses
goodbye to their song and flutter
i'm breaking up with mascara   blue jeans
and long texts   i give my notice   letters
of acceptance   rejection   indifference
take it down   off the hands of the jury
the decision or prognosis can stay unread
break me where i was first broken
where each day begs annihilation   old love
new love   don't look for me   flap
on regret   guilt   despair
you want an elegy for a dying year
before you feel the weight
of the world without it

that magic won't cast

Poem to the Body

When you finally die, darling,
the wound remains open, so
you return to it. The last winds blow
down the door of your dream house
as you return to the blood
that came early, to the site you
pried him off you, back to the places
no one is allowed to touch, even out of love,
back to the playground where you were spat on,
the homeroom you were bent over,
the primary halls you were chased down,
the lonely offices and exam rooms where
what mattered was measured against you and gosh,
the inordinate number of dressing rooms.

You will return to the streets of broad daylight, where you were hyper-visible
to the I've-got-something-for-you-big-girl fat-fuck-of-it-all,
maybe it was a hospital room, a gymnasium
or a cemetery where you said goodbye to the ones you loved,
or the studio apartment where the phone rang
with the news, your unanswered grief ringing through.

When you return to the age where you learned
of the pain ushered into the world with you,
and the rooms you watched them suffer rage
and age, when you return to the years
you were instructed to be less, as you were too much,
always too much, girl you're too much to ever
know enough.

When you return to the disappointment of loving
people who never loved you, who followed your cues,
you have arrived at the wound. Do not drink from it.
The perimeter will remain unchanged but the eye,

a dark blue you can't take with you. My love,
when you return to the world of first sin
and true regret, the pain will be pulled out
of you like you were once pulled: perhaps headfirst
or breech, by your shoulders, long way or short,
you were pulled whole into this wailing world.

Trash Day

I schedule one day a year for self-pity,
my own lonely Christmas. There won't be any
meditation when I wake up, alone or with someone.

We will gather 'round the mirror and weep, so loudly
the baby next door will wail back. Its mother too. *Damn,*

we will cry out into the insurmountable, cowed by shame
that there is so much beauty
we do not know. Love, unearned. Grace, unpractised.

We will recall harm we have witnessed. Cruelty,
carried. Indifference, we with privilege, ignored. Today,
we don't promise to do better or be anything.

Sorry, there will be no volta here. Outside, the pigeon
we don't feed scurries about our rubbish, hungry
to make nothing of its discoveries, but a meal.

Flower Embroidery / Womxn's Work

My friends keep dying and I bear no children
again and again and maybe tomorrow

I feel like dying, maybe
I get up. Maybe go back to sleep

so attentive to the breath of the dead, I can feel
my name on my neck, lifting off me like a fingerprint,

which is a white metaphor for guilt. After the body,
the name is the first binding agent to what

I could be convinced is the soul: an excess of soul
is my inhumanity, as I have been known to squander,

time, opportunities, trust. All I destroy, simultaneously
bound to and lifting off me, like night lifts its hand

to the wailing mouth of day, my failures always surprise me.
My will rolls off across the chiton leaf of me

where I was first bifurcated, then joined
by a love divine. The instrument of the needle

is usually precise, even if the outcome appears illegible,
and sloppy. This hour, the sob of me crescendos in my lungs

and this piece of thread that the needle has sewn through
me whispers, like the song of a secret army. Silken grief

finally come to rescue me.

When I Dream of Escape,

the voice of God says: *Bitch,*
wake up! Why are you
sleeping? I gave you a whole
life and entire earth of dirt! What
is you doing? She hollers: *Don't*
make me come down there. Finish
your work. Don't be careless.
When she proclaims, *I'm giving you*
three hours, I know I have three hours.

To live like this, under the threat
of your own existence, your pink tongue
lapping at the far side of the bowl,
your neck fur drenched in your own
frailty and so much water. There is
no other God. No other order. No other place.

Found God Poem

There is no God but God
Thank God
God of that's what you get
God who don't like ugly
Lord above
Lord have mercy
mercy, mercy me
As God is my witness
I have loved my neighbour,
have broken bread and yet—
God whose eye is on the sparrow
whose eye I fear
For the love of God
Omnipotent Lord and Saviour
hear my prayers
Lord help us
God forsaken
God who is the greatest
God who saves queens
Will it
God only knows
where I'd be without you
what I did to deserve this
God of my understanding
who works in mysterious ways
show yourself
It's showtime
All Glory unto God
God in heaven
In which we trust
Oh God
Oh God
Forgive me
My God, please, please, please, please, please, please, please, please

God of my promises and frailties
God who helps those who help themselves
who sits silent in the room where it happens
God damn
Which God did I offend
show me
The Act of God
So help me God

III. PIANO

Dark Hallelujah

The dark soles of Gregory Hines' tap, across the Apollo
    Mid-dark, like Mahalia's midnight alto for Martin

Dark water, where the wave returns to the sea, from where it rises
    Deep-dark where it roils, raptures and gently speaks thunder

Coiled tight, as the flight of the water dancer's pointed toe when it flexes
    Dark as the thigh closing the gap

Black, as in no need for precedence, firsts so irrelevant,
    the melody sprinting beneath the lyrics, the beauty omnipotent

Dark as the pleasures yet to be named, what remains undiscovered
    The darkness that draws you so near, for a moment we all disappear

So dark no one knocks on my door when the lights are out
    Dark-skinned, as in the secret universe that exists between us

        The joy, all for us

Tightly coiled, as the Black belt of the choral refrain, again and again
    Coiled like the corners of your heart's labyrinth, mama

The dark mass of the pendulum as it swings, unmeasured, through space

    The sun doesn't blaze without the infinite twirl of its dark skirts,
the undershine of its belly telling the Black croon of its broil

    Tightly coiled, like the vine let go the grape
Coiled dark, as in within striking distance

Black like the back of the bus on the way to the Museum of Natural History,
    when Marcus sang *Lift Every Voice and Sing*, and Nathan started crunking

and Natasha pulled out her eurythmy moves, so Lakeisha got beat-boxing
and I wanted to join in drumming, but just watched, my Black pupils,
humming

Kiese Says, *Black People Deserve Beautiful Sentences*, but a Fragment is the Best I Can Do / Songbook for the Names I Have Been Called

I might be
The most beautiful *Black bitch* you've ever seen
The *least original* sunrise

I might be
darker than the dark velvet of the moon

Might be the slow *creep* of comfort edging you back
Might be joy's *affirmative* call to *action*

Be the huckleberry grown *fat, fuck* with sweetness
Be the *ugly* moan of pleasure bust open

Be
As *lopsided* as the bountiful branch of the fruiting tree

More *fragile* than the silence of untroubled water
Trouble, trouble, trouble, trouble
I might be

Dear Reader,

I know the pain of trying to keep pace with light,
the desire to become visible to one solely invested
in my initial darkness. I know it's a matter of
minutes before the hot tea cools.

Do you know how it feels to be picked, like a dress,
to accentuate someone else's beauty, to be the thing
against which someone else can glow, to be the
marker, the palate cleanser, the one who knows
their place and holds still. Holds tight. Smiles.
Do you know how to do this? Have you
chosen the company of those you thought wouldn't
outpace you. Those who would keep you company
during your midnight hours. The desire for a fat
hug from a friend fat with time.

We have worn the day like an eye mask, over our
slumber. We understand the underside of the day.
We have known the simultaneity of collapse and banquet.
We have read Lucille Clifton together and wept.
We have turned to Rita Dove and the page after
a long goodbye. We have looked to Vievee Francis
to help bear the truth of our own mothers.
Of our own knowing. And found joy. And found
sorrow. And found moments of unlocking. We wear
the years of our childhoods like found keys around
a cluttered keyring. We have examined the dark imperative
to survive. Let us consider, the difference between
who we are and who we say we are. That the principle
behind how we name our gods is also the distance
between you and I.

Last Days of Summer

Today I won't write poems about yesterday, only your face,
plums, jam on bread and butter. The pitch of pleasure that presents
itself like weeping. My love, even here, in our pied-à-terre, we can't
escape dark waters. We row the canal, beneath the Bridge of Sighs,
taking turns looking forward. Perhaps,
if this poem were the bowl of pears, persimmons and pomegranates,
on the table pushed flush against my sternum, pinning me to my seat
in this Italian heat, we might never grow old, plying each other all day
with reasons to devour. Desire must be chewed before it's consumed,
fingered by the soft pads of want. On this plate, I need only balance
the sweet with the savoury, the ratio of pepper to oil. Today we are alive
in summer. Unencumbered. Tomorrow hangs like the apricots from the tree just
outside the window. Let the wind choose our fate. Come, cook with me.
Today, the only question: do we choose yoghurt or cream.

Constraint

I love writers' bodies, their subtle
        reluctancies to the usual persuasions.

Tired arguments,
        on behalf of the beach or the gym,

fail to coax them
        as much as the gaze

of the unblinking moon.
        Humble shoulders hide

beneath sweaters, robes
        silk if you're lucky.

I love the heavy slopes
        of their fronts, when hunched

over a desk
        or adjacent to a window,

facing the city or country,
        framing the village or occupied territory.

Eyes noisy and darting,
        steady and open or milky and closed,

There are a glory of angles
        crocked teeth,

a blank jaw, a well-groomed limp,

and oh their hips—
        pushing past possibility and precedent

My body's beauty,

just another wonky outline in a chorus.

Self-Portrait as a Queer Block Party

Your fat spills soft across the moonlit crown of grass.
Your soul mates are a gaggle of fish, shoaling thick,
until you are schooled enough in this love.
The hours left before sunrise are shimmering scales, marked
for the net, long-cast // before you learned time had an end //
Bodies so true, joy pools behind the ears & around the clavicles
like jewels. Like fucking jewels. Pores chant in the street:
we are alive. Speakers blast the humid sky like firecrackers
in June. You take the first hand, then hip, with you through the dance,
glide, until you find the body you abandoned // measurements ago //
You travel it with your partner. Their unshaved armpits, bleached
seaweed-green. Their bare midriff, a silk thicket. Their saffron robe, a
protection against the binary of day or night. An inch of belly
leaps beyond your shirt, like a flying fish in silver light.

Kindness changes the light in here, dusts off the old innocence. Can you remember the best compliment you've ever received? Of course you can. Aren't we always yearning to feel that way again. For the again. What is restoration, but a promise kept? A small searching and the relief found at the bottom of the junk drawer. Ticket tucked into the jacket pocket. The text message from the person you love, telling you that they love you: that they're thinking of you and holding what you love within them.

NOTES

"Bang and a Whimper": In full, the T.S. Eliot quote from the last line of *The Hollow Men* reads, "*Not with a bang but a whimper.*"

"Homosexual": The definition used in this poem is a paraphrase from *Oxford Languages* dictionary.

"Triolet": The repeating phrase in this poem is taken from the first line of an untitled poem by E. E. Cummings, published in Poetry, January 1939, Vol. LIII, No. IV.

"Sonnet of the Bull": The epigraph is taken from a Facebook lead-in to online article by Caroline Mortimer, titled "Bull kills itself after horns set on fire at Spanish fiesta" *The Independent* July 26, 2017. The italacised phrase is from the penultimate couplet is from article, proper. There exists an accompanying video.

"In Lieu of Ode": The final tercet is taken from the acceptance speech for the Community Change Agent Award, from Tarana Burke, at the *Black Girls Rock* awards show on BET, Aug 26 2018.

"Said Sorrow to Joy": The poem references Kahlil Gibran's poem, *On Joy and Sorrow*, published in *The Prophet* (Knopf, 1923).

"Bodies Like Oceans": The title is taken from the social media hashtag created by the photographer and visual artist, Shoog McDaniels.

"Tides": An italicised phrase in this poem is taken from Leonard Cohen's title song from the album, *You Want it Darker*, released in 2016. In full, the quote reads, *You want it darker / We kill the flame*.

"Pier 52": Inspiration from this poem is taken from the photography retrospective, *The Life and Times of Alvin Baltrop*, presented by the Bronx Museum of Art, in May 2019.

"Black Art Sonnet in Which Lines Were Shuffled and Glued": Poem commissioned and presented by the Cave Canem Foundation, at The Brooklyn Museum Target's First Saturdays Pop-Up Poetry celebration of the *Soul of a Nation: Art in the Age of Black* Poetry exhibition, organised by Tate Modern and curated by Ashley James.

"Ars Diaspora with Drinking Gourd": Some language in this poem is borrowed from *Follow the Drinking Gourd*, by Richie Havens.

"Got 'Til It's Gone": This poem references the Mark Romanek music video for the song of the same title, by Janet Jackson, Joni Mitchell and Q-Tip.

"Museum of What is Owed": Poem references a quote from Audre Lorde's address, *Learning from the 60s*, delivered at Harvard University, in celebration of Malcolm X Weekend, February 1982.

"notebook full of thirst for the new year": Poem written after *evening and my once dead husband*, by Lucille Clifton.

"Found God Poem": The poem uses cultural and / or religious expressions of God, found in common parlance.

"Dark Hallelujah": The poem references the reported friendship between Dr. Martin Luther King Jr. and the gospel singer and vocal artist, Mahalia Jackson, who was known to sing to him before his orations.

"Kiese Says, *Black People Deserve Beautiful Sentences*, but a Fragment is the Best I Can Do / Songbook for the Names I Have Been Called": In full, the Kiese Laymon quote from the social media platform, Twitter, on October 29, 2020, 4:43 PM reads, "Black people deserve beautiful sentences. We really really do."

Unremarkably, my affinity for art began early. I dove into it. My work is influenced by every poet, painter, piner, crooner, strummer, troubadour who told their truth their way: who wrote, painted, crooned, directed, sculpted, acted, composed, edited or tapped their way into the cannon, or danced around it, or stubbornly toiled beside it. With what my mother refers to as the "big eyes" of my childhood, I devoured everything. Dead and living, you taught me from afar. Anyone with the courage to claim a dream, even if you were never recognised for it, even if you never had the opportunity to pursue it. You, who perhaps channeled that energy into other pursuits or people. Perhaps you pummeled yourself with your own dream. Perhaps you always knew your dream, but sometimes you waver. I have wavered too. This one is for you. You are present in this work. Your dream dreamed my dream. This, our collaboration.

ACKNOWLEDGMENTS

A bouquet of gratitude for the editors of the following journals and anthologies, in which the poems in this book, sometimes in earlier versions, first appeared:

Academy of American Poets Poem-a-Day: "Half Girl, Then Elegy," "Pier 52" and "A Flair for Language"

American Chordata: "Exhibition of the Queered Woman"

BOMB Magazine: "Homosexual" and "Moving to Brooklyn During the Peak of a Pandemic"

Crab Fat Magazine: "The Butcher: A Love Poem" and "Allāhu Akbar: | for my body | under the rule | of white supremacy"

Coffee House Press: "Tripartite"

Columbia Journal: "notebook full of thirst for the new year"

Cosmonauts Avenue: "Three Women / Two Transfers and a Token / One Reincarnation"

Guernica: "Closure"

Gulf Coast: "Dark Hallelujah," "Got 'Til It's Gone," "Direct Objects," and "Flower Embroidery / Womxn's Work"

Lambda Literary: "In Lieu of Ode"

Literary Hub: "Wall"

Logger, The Believer: "Bodies Like Oceans"

Los Angeles Review of Books: "Sonnet of the Bull"

Nat.Brut: "the only rooms I occupy | are empty"

Newtown Literary: "Tides"

No Dear: "When I said I had Obamacare, what I meant was *Medicaid*"

No Tokens: "Self-Portrait as a Queer Block Party"

Poetry Magazine: "Autobiography of Thud," "First Kiss / Under Capitalism" and "My Mother is a shot—"

Poetry Society of America: "Proverb"

REDIVIDER: "Ceremony"

The Arkansas International: "The Good News"

The Coil: "Things | I know to be true, | but will never prove"

The Common: "After the Last Calorie of the Apocalypse / Prayer for the Clinically Obese"

The Felt: "Whereas"

The Nation: "Proper Fat"

The Paris Review (online): "Promise"

The Recluse: "Prologue to a Name," "Ice Sculpture" and "Mama Wata"

The Rumpus: "More"

The Yale Review: "Ars Diaspora with Drinking Gourd"

Vast Magazine: "Heaven Be a Sturdy Chair" and "Last Days of Summer"

Wildness: "What We Leave Undone"

Winter Tangerine: "Haircut"

A version of "Poem to Watch Over You" was featured in an online exhibition, *First Made Into Language*, curated by PJ Gubatina Policarpio, for Southern Exposure.

Black Lesbians—We Are the Revolution by Sinister Wisdom: "Mirror Talk"

Emerge by Lambda Literary: "Abecedarian for Leaving"

The Other Side of Violet by Great Weather for Media: "Fruit Flies"

"Wall" and "In Lieu of Ode" were reprinted in Dream of the River, by Jacar Press. "Half Girl, Then Elegy" was reprinted in *Embodied: An Intersectional Feminist Comics Poetry Anthology* by A Wave Blue World. "Self-Portrait as a Queer Block Party" was reprinted in *Already Felt: VOLUME I*, by Raptor press. "What We Leave Undone" was reprinted in *Best Small Fictions*, by Sonder press. "What We Leave Undone" was reprinted in *Islands Are but Mountains*, by Platypus Press.

A number of these poems were included in a chapbook, *Daughter Tongue*, published by African Poetry Book (Akashic Books, 2018). Several were included in a manuscript that received a Discovery Poetry Prize from the Unterberg Poetry Center of the 92NY.

Acknowledgement is due to the following for their support:

Thank you to the educational systems that cultivated my love of learning and shaped my perceptions of the world. Thank you to the publishers, artists and art administrators who steward the work and embrace the merit of my project. Thank you for your generous support: Westbury Friends School, Friends Academy, Hofstra University, the Academy of American Poets, the Home School, Winter Tangerine, the Binders, New York University, the Cave Canem Foundation, Lambda Literary, the African Poetry Book Fund, the 92NY Unterberg Poetry Center, Newtown Literary, No Tokens, Tin House, the Bread Loaf Writers' Conference, the Palm Beach Poetry Festival, the Seventh Wave, the New York Foundation of the Arts, the Cafe Royal Cultural Foundation, the New York City Department of Cultural Affairs, Coffee House Press, Kweli Journal, Association for Size Diversity and Health and the Poetry Foundation.

Thank you to my contemporaries with whom I share the field. You have my deepest respect and admiration. Special thank you to old cohort and new: Gbenga Adesina, Alfredo Aguilar, Kaveh Akbar, Kemi Alabi, Sarah Ghazal Ali, Moncho Alvarado, Ally Ang, Leah Angstman, Raymond Antrobus, Cameron Awkward-Rich, Trinity Babe, Desiree C. Bailey, Jamica Baldwin, Sasha Banks, Rick Barot, Lisa Marie Basile, Ellen Bass, S. Erin Batiste, Jan Beatty, Yasmin Belkhyr, Oliver Baez Bendorf, Jari Bradley, Elizabeth Bryant, Bryan Byrdlong, Celeste Chan, Wo Chan, Celeste Chan, Cortney Lamar Charleston, Alex Chee, Joyce Chen, Kirsten Shu-ying Chen, Wendy Chin-Tanner, Franny Choi, Tiana Clark, Ama Codjoe, Rio Cortez, Nicole Dickson, Timothy Donnelly, Rita Dove, An Duplan, Saddiq M. Dzukogi, Carolina Ebeid, Joshua Escobar, J. Jennifer Espinoza, Bernardine Evaristo, Eve Ewing, Logan February, Bernard Ferguson, Lydia Flores, Tim Fredrick, Ziwe Fumudoh, Benjamin Garcia, Roxane Gay, Hafizah Geter, Aracelis Girmay, Nicholas Goodly, Adjua Gargi Nzinga Greaves, Garth Greenwell, Rachel Eliza Griffiths, Joy Harjo, Maliha Hashmi, Deborah Hauser, Marwa Helal, Laura Henriksen, Jon Paul Higgins, Lauren Hilger, JP Howard, Marie Howe, Luther Hughes, Erica Hunt, Lauren Hunter, Híl Davis de Ince, and Vicki Iorio, Major Jackson, Mira Jacobs, Randa Jarrar, Nicole Shawan Junior, Donika Kelly, Ted Kerr, Willie L. Kinard, Rosamond S. King, Sloka Krishnan, Stephon Lawrence,

Eugenia Leigh, Alison Lewis, Jiaoyang Li, Zefyr Lisowski, Kyle Carrero Lopez, J. Estanislao Lopez, Nadra Mabrouk, Nadra Mabrouk, T Kira Madden, Terese Marie Mailhot, Randall Mann, Maya Marshall, Charleen McClure, Coco Mellors, Lynn Melnick, Elizabeth Metzger, Yesenia Montilla, Ebony S. Murphy, Matthew Nathan, Nkosi Nkululeko, Naomi Shihab Nye, Natasha Oladokun, Matthew Olzmann, Leila Ortiz, Wendy C. Ortiz, Dustin Pearson, Sarah Perry, Xan Phillips, Alycia Pirmohamed, the Pohos, Karisma Price, C. Russell Price, Joy Priest, C. Quintana, Shivanee N. Ramlochan, Claudia Rankine, Brett Rawson, Roger Reeves, Bükem Reitmayer, Sarah Sala, Sonia Sanchez, Nicole Sealey, Diamond Sharp, Christina Sharpe, Michael Shayan, Jackie Sherbow, Warsan Shire, Angela Simione, Imogen Xtian Smith, Patricia Smith, Pamela Sneed, Layli Long Soldier, Erika Stevens, Stacy Szymaszek, Malcolm Tariq, Daniel Tay, Brandon Taylor, Courtney Faye Taylor, Ricky Tucker, Leah Umansky, Joanna C. Valente, Daniel Vida, Vanessa Angélica Villarreal, Nikki Wallschlaeger, Simone White, Phillip B. Williams, Katie Willingham, Keith S. Wilson, Jane Wong, Alex Yip, Kamelya Omayma Youssef, Samantha Zighelboim.

Thank you to the following authors for revealing what is possible on the page: Chinua Achebe, Gwendolyn Brooks, Lucille Clifton, Kahlil Gibran, bell hooks, June Jordan, Audre Lorde, Toni Morrison, Rainer Maria Rilke, Jalāl al-Dīn Muḥammad Rūmī.

Thank you to my teachers and professors who reached into themselves to inspire something new within me. Bread of my bread. Who urged me to interrogate my positionality to my art and the greater world. Who urged me to take my craft seriously: Mr. Austin, Samiya Bashir, Simon Bridges, Marie Buono, Gregory Djanikian, Vievee Francis, Terrance Hayes, Ninso John High, Annette Kern, Yusef Komunyakaa, Joseph O. Legaspi, Phillis Levin, Robin Coste Lewis. Gregory Pardlo, Camille Rankine, TC Tolbert, Lewis Warsh, Monica Youn. Thank you, Sharon Olds, for your exemplar tenderness and generosity, which informs all my poems (and thank you for giving me the best compliment of my little life). Thank you to Deborah Landau for signing off on my thesis! Thank you to Toi Derricotte and Cornelius Eady for the dream of Cave Canem. Thank you to Chris Abani and Kwame Dawes for the vision of the African Poetry Book Fund.

Thank you to Melissa Febos, Kiese Laymon and dearest Jericho Brown, for lighting my candle from your own. Thank you for taking the time to read my work and for your generous words, which usher this book into the world. Most of all, thank you for your work.

Thank you to the entire team at Alice James Books, for believing in and publishing this work. Thank you to Nectar Literary for carrying the torch. Most especially, thank you to Carey Salerno, for your notes, patience and grace.

Thank you to the tremendously talented Noma Osula, for seeing the world the way you do, and for blessing the cover of this collection with borrowed and spectacular beauty.

Thank you to Idra Novey for your excellent example of literary citizenship and your kind heart.

Thank you again, Kiese, for carrying the message, through you good work, good words and good deeds. Thank you for believing in me, immediately and utterly. You are the definition of family.

Thank you to my guides, spirits, muses, ancestors and to those I am and unable to name here.

To anyone who has ever hired me, recommended me for a gig, carried my name into a room, loaned me money or given it freely, bought me a meal, given me a hug, a compliment, a pep talk. To those unnamable who read, teach, support and make space for my poems, thank you. To my clients and students who have been my greatest teachers, thank you. I am still learning.

Thank you to my beloveds who spoke daylight into my evening hours during the hours and years of writing this book; to Laura Pendleton Buccieri, for being the first reader of so many of these poems; to Ky Hamilton, for your unending love and support; to Bruce Entin, for sharing this journey; to DéLana R.A. Dameron, for your rigorous honesty, generosity and being a bomb-ass Black woman; to Candace Williams, for your constancy, generous advice and brilliance; to Sarah Kaplan Gould, for the blessing of your friendship; to Sahar Romani, for your sisterhood and poem chats; to Ricardo Alberto Maldonado, por ser el hermano y mentor que necesitaba; to Jennifer Villafuerte, sestra, look at us here on the other side. "We did it Joe!"

Thank you to the fat futurists who make space for my work and my person. Who make the world a safer, more gorgeous and more welcoming space: Farizah Ahmad, Farizah Ahmad, Angel Austin, Ash Nischuk, Angel Austin, Shoog McDaniel, Shoog McDaniel, Ash Nischuk.

Thank you to the communities of all my intersections, but especially to Black people. Thank God for Black people. For every place we exist. On the continent and within the diaspora. For the universe between us. For the universe within us. For the limitlessness when we see each other.

If I have forgotten anyone, it is only because you are a part of me.

Most importantly, thank you to my family:

Thank you to my father for nurturing my relationship art. For your passion for art, culture and philosophy. For gifting me my first art supplies and favourite books, with which I would create my own healing.

Thank you to my brother for sharing your childhood with me and pursuing your dreams alongside mine.

Thank you to my mother for being the first Black woman to ever love me. For being extraordinary. For being powerful. For speaking power into me. For providing me the tools to craft language on my own terms. Thank you for supporting my dreams, having no idea where they might lead me. Thank you for your courage. My art thanks you. Lives in you.

I thank God for allowing me to conceive this work.

ment pigeon's unmarked death
during the walk I made, as a reluctant
promise. I pitched it 'round
my lover's throat and found
a synonym for loss. I lobbed it
with the tenderness I would have
parted my child's locks.
I hurled the circle to the sky and
dove though gravity with raised arms.
I rolled my hips front and back,
until the music rose like steam.
I slipped my body, like a dress
made with someone else in mind,
turning back with wide wonder,
to gaze at what remained. I
shucked the ego with one fist
of wind and hard rain.
I whispered into my beloved's ear,
Here we go again.

Epilogue
(Hidden Track)

I flung the circle of my life
over the chair's back because
the day was done and I'd barely
started. I tossed it over the pave-

Recent Titles from Alice James Books

Alice James Books is committed to publishing books that matter. The press was founded in 1973 in Boston, Massachusetts to give women access to publishing. As a cooperative, authors performed the day-to-day undertakings of the press. The press continues to expand and grow from its formative roots, guided by its founding values of access, excellence, inclusivity, and collaboration in publishing. Its mission is to publish books that matter and preserve a place of belonging for poets who inspire us. AJB seeks to broaden our collective interpretation of what constitutes the American poetic voice and is dedicated to helping its artists achieve purposeful engagement with broad audiences and communities nationwide. The press was named for Alice James, sister to William and Henry, whose extraordinary gift for writing went unrecognized during her lifetime.

Designed by Tiani Kennedy

Printed by Sheridan Saline